The Weil Lectures on American Citizenship
of The University of North Carolina

*PROBLEMS OF DEMOCRACY IN
LATIN AMERICA*

The Weil Lectures on American Citizenship

JACOB H. HOLLANDER
American Citizenship and Economic Welfare

R. GOODWYN RHETT
The Progress of American Ideals

WILLIAM BENNETT MUNRO
Personality in Politics

EDWARD ALSWORTH ROSS
Roads to Social Peace

WILLIAM ALLEN WHITE
Some Cycles of Cathay

HENRY NOBLE MACCRACKEN
John the Common Weal

WILLIAM HEARD KILPATRICK
Our Educational Task

HAROLD J. LASKI
Democracy in Crisis

GEORGE NORLIN
Fascism and Citizenship

FELIX FRANKFURTER
The Commerce Clause

HENRY A. WALLACE
Technology Corporations, and the General Welfare

T. V. SMITH
Discipline for Democracy

GALO PLAZA
Problems of Democracy in Latin America

CHAPEL HILL: THE UNIVERSITY OF NORTH CAROLINA PRESS

PROBLEMS OF DEMOCRACY

IN LATIN AMERICA

By

GALO PLAZA
PRESIDENT OF ECUADOR, 1948-1952

Chapel Hill
THE UNIVERSITY OF NORTH CAROLINA PRESS

Copyright, 1955, by
The University of North Carolina Press

Manufactured in the United States of America

PREFACE

ON OCCASION over the years, the University of North Carolina has invited eminent persons from other nations to deliver the annual Weil Lectures on American Citizenship. If justification for this seeming discrepancy is needed, it lies in the belief that a visitor enjoys perspective, and perspective can improve understanding, and also in the increasing concern that citizens of the United States have with affairs beyond their own borders.

Galo Plaza has devoted his life to the Republic of Ecuador. A practical farmer in a predominantly agricultural country, he has studied and applied ways to wiser and more productive land use. As a citizen in a nation of great social distances, he has championed respect for the dignity of the individual and liberal government on behalf of all people. And as the inheritor of a long tradition of public responsibility—his father became his nation's president—he has served as mayor of the captial city of Quito, as minister of national defense, as ambassador to Washington, and as president of Ecuador from 1948 to 1952.

Mr. Plaza understands profoundly the differences

that divide us, the mutual interests that unite us, and the limitless opportunities before us in the Western Hemisphere. It is a privilege to make available to a wider audience his observations on these matters made in Chapel Hill in the spring of 1954.

>Alexander Heard, Chairman
>Committee on Established Lectures

CONTENTS

Preface   v

I
North and South Americans—A Comparison   1

II
Ecuador—An Experiment in Democracy   20

III
Democracy in Latin America—Past and Present   43

*PROBLEMS OF DEMOCRACY IN
LATIN AMERICA*

CHAPTER I

NORTH AND SOUTH AMERICANS— A COMPARISON

In 1946, at the Commencement Exercises of the University of Maryland, I tried to convey something with which I had been preoccupied and which bears repeating today. I spoke along these lines:

Throughout its history this nation (the United States) has molded a philosophy of life based on the principles and ideals for which the country was founded. This way of life, that for the rest of the world is not more than a distant aspiration, was taken by succeeding generations of Americans as a matter of fact. Many times people lost sight of how this precious treasure had been attained and what it meant. They had not to fight for it or to defend it, they did not know what it meant to live without it, it was taken for granted. But today this new generation coming out into the world can no longer take security as a matter of fact. If you want to preserve your most cherished possession, your way of life, you will have to be, from now on, alert and ready to protect it. To be able to preserve democracy in a changing world we should start by changing our state of mind from that of believing that the world we know is secure and beyond destruction. You must realize that postwar times have brought a challenge to your institutions, that danger exists, and that these same institutions need and deserve protection, for without them the era of the United States, the era of America, will pass, not after centuries like the Greek and Roman eras, but in a period of time that in the perspective of history would mean no more than a flash.

What has to be contrived so that the Americas can play the part that destiny has preordained for them? How can the United States, as a world leader, fully assume the role of guardian of the people's ideals that inspire the American way of life?

Should not the other half of the hemisphere, what is called Latin America, be a militant and powerful ally in the great crusade against the forces that seek to undermine our spiritual values? Could not the whole hemisphere constitute an inner bastion for democracy?

Would it be wise to let poverty, ignorance, disease, injustice, and propaganda breed communism in Latin America, so that instead of a powerful ally she became the vulnerable under-belly? What can be effected from within and without the continent so that millions of people who dream of a better life, to which they have an inherent right, can live in an atmosphere of political liberties?

I shall strive, in the course of these lectures, to explain that in spite of historical, economic, racial, psychological, and cultural differences between the people of the north and those of the south of the hemisphere, there are deeper analogies which stem from the fact that we are all children of the New World, with less than five centuries of Western civilization and two of independent government in our historical make-up, so that we do not have to bridge great abysses in seeking solutions to our problems—it is simply a matter of understanding each other and trying to know more about one another with no more impressive a weapon than an open mind.

Later I will relate to you a personal experience, how as president of Ecuador I had the privilege of helping my country in what could be considered an experiment in true and militant democracy; how the experiment did not blow up in my face even though we were dealing with supposedly explosive elements, poverty and a record of political instability hard to match anywhere in a politically unstable continent; and how the people learned from experience what cherished possessions liberty and respect for human rights are and why it is worth while to protect and defend, and fight, if necessary, so as not to lose those newly acquired rights.

And, finally, we will lift our sights to the panorama of the whole continent and see how deeply democracy is entrenched in the heart of the people; what should and could be accomplished by making the Ecuadoran experiment available to other lands where people have been deprived of justice and liberty, have been oppressed and submerged in darkness by political tyrannies that should have no place on American soil; and as a conclusion, we shall see what you, our friends and neighbors, can do to help us and by so doing help yourselves.

Much has been said about these problems of mutual interest and I am afraid there is not much that I can add to the many learned opinions from both ends of our hemisphere. The difference between what I have to say and what many others have already said is that while most have looked at the problem from their own point of view and analyzed it and understood it according to their own experience and cultural background, I am in a position to look at the situation from both sides of the fence. You might ask me, why?

I am a true Latin American, from many generations back. My father's parents fled from political persecution in Colombia, because they were liberal, and his ancestors fought in the Wars of Independence with distinction. On my mother's side we have been in Quito since the sixteenth century, so you can see that my roots are deeply imbedded in Ecuadoran soil. On the other hand, from my experiences as a student in the United States I learned to admire and love this great nation of yours and always dreamt that knowledge and understanding of both our cultural backgrounds could bring about a powerful democratic America that would become a beacon for the world to follow.

South of the Rio Grande there are twenty independent countries, some large like Brazil, larger than the continental United States; some of medium size like Colombia, as large as all the Atlantic Coast states from Maine through Florida plus West Virginia and Ohio; some small like El Salvador, no larger than Vermont and Connecticut combined. These countries do not represent a single political, ethnical, or economic unit; on the contrary, there exists an ample range of differences. Politically, Uruguay is a true democracy, as pure and unadulterated as can be found anywhere. At the other end, one country is practically the private property of a single man. Ten of the twenty countries are democracies, some more so, some less; two are in a period of transition toward democracy; eight are dictatorships.

Only Costa Rica, Argentina, Chile, and Uruguay are predominantly European in their racial make-up. Brazil and several countries in the Caribbean region have an important Negro population. Mexico, Guatemala, and the Andean countries have a large and valuable Indian and Indo-Hispanic element in their population.

In most of our countries Spanish is spoken; in Brazil, with the largest population of all, Portuguese is the language; in Haiti, French is spoken. In some countries dialects are frequently heard; in Bolivia the Quechua, in Paraguay the Guarani, and in some areas in Mexico vernacular Indian dialects are widely used even by foreign peddlers.

Economically all the Latin American countries are

largely producers of raw materials; industries have progressed notably during the last few decades, but we are not as industrialized as we want to be and should be. Most of our economy is of a tropical nature which complements that of the United States. Those countries in the temperate zone compete with the United States, as in the case of Argentina. As in no other Latin American country, immigration and a rich, flat, temperate area have given Argentina a background much like that of the United States, and competition has contributed in establishing relations with the United States on a basis that in some cases has brought about misunderstandings.

Let us compare the historical background of the United States and of Latin America. The Spanish American republics are the progeny of a colonial system set up by an absolute monarch who ruled in the name of the Catholic Church. After the Wars of Independence, in the early nineteenth century, the people, without any previous experience in self-government, found themselves unprepared to face their new responsibilities. The divisions and subdivisions of the old viceroyalties, presidencies of "audiencias," and other colonial political departments developed into as many republics; each one took with it a heritage of political turmoil which logically bred dictatorships and brought about oppression for great majorities of heterogeneous human elements which in many cases have not found the road to stable representative government even to this day.

The case of Brazil is somewhat different. Brazil

was colonized by the Portuguese. The government of the mother country, headed by the emperor himself, came over from Europe when Napoleon invaded Portugal in 1808. Brazil was an empire as late as 1889. In any case her people had the same lack of experience and background for democratic government that the Spanish Americans had.

The English colonies in North America were governed for the most part under charters which were democratic constitutions. The first settlers had fled from religious persecution in Europe and organized their new communities on the basis of freedom and tolerance. The constitution drawn up in Philadelphia was the logical culmination of a process that had been going on for a long time. Your background of government was the exact opposite of that of Latin America. From here stems the strength of your institutions and the weakness of ours.

Our respective developments up to the end of the nineteenth century did not parallel, but offered a curious pattern. At the time of the discovery of the New World the indigenous population of what is now the United States was primitive and nomadic, while to the south existed the remarkably enlightened civilizations of the Aztecs, Mayas, and Incas in Mexico, Central America, and what is today Colombia, Ecuador, Peru, Bolivia, Chile, and northern Argentina.

The pilgrims arrived in Plymouth 128 years after the founding of the first white settlement in Santo

Domingo. New York was a village of 200 when Potosí in Bolivia had 100,000 inhabitants. About 1650 the white population of the English colonies increased to 85,000 while the non-indigenous population of Latin America was over 2,000,000. When New York City had 14,000 inhabitants in 1750, Mexico City numbered 90,000. In 1790, no more than five cities in North America had more than 5,000 inhabitants each, while in Latin America at least ten had more than 20,000. At the time the United States became independent there were 3,900,000 inhabitants and at the same period in Latin America there were 20,000,000. During the nineteenth century, expansion and immigration brought amazing growth to the United States while Latin America remained stationary. In 1870 the United States with 38,500,000 inhabitants had 500,000 more than Latin America. At the end of the century the population was 76,000,000 in the United States and 63,000,000 in Latin America.[1]

What happened to Latin America after such a running start? Many factors favored progress in the northern part of the hemisphere and retarded it in the south—above all, political stability. While your young and great nation was hacking its way west in search of new horizons under a stable, representative government, our countries were the victims of their inexperience and

[1] Figures quoted from Carlos Dávila, *Nosotros, los de las Américas*, Editorial del Pacífico, Santiago de Chile, 1950, pp. 306-314.

the people were wasting their time and energy, and losing their lives in sterile struggles of a political nature.

This was not, of course, the only reason. The eternal struggle of man versus nature was not as cruel and hard in the great valleys, cut by slow, navigable rivers and with a climate similar to that of Europe, as it was in the lofty Andean valleys or the teeming jungles where the white European had great difficulty in readjusting. It was only logical, then, that the restless masses of people in Europe moved to the temperate lands of North America. They also came later to the temperate zone of South America, Argentina, Uruguay, and Chile, where they made a great contribution to the progress of these countries, but there again, distances were greater from Europe than they were to New York, port of entry of most of the immigrant flow to North America.

There are fewer differences of climate and environment between southern Sweden and, say, Minnesota, thousands of miles away, than between a cool valley in the Andes, some 7,000 or 8,000 feet above the sea, and the tropical lands at sea level no more than a hundred miles away. It is easier for a Swede to move to the Middle West and readjust himself, without major difficulties, than it is for an Ecuadoran farmer in the Andes to move to the exuberant, rich volcanic soil at the foot of the Cordillera, closer to the ocean, but where the conditions of life differ so much from his native environment that readjustment becomes a major ordeal. In the case of the Swede he is moving horizontally within the temperate zone; in the case of the Ecuadoran farmer he is going from conditions which are very similar to those of the temperate zone to an entirely new environment in the tropics. We could call his migration vertical.

You can now see how geography has favored the North and conspired against the South. Your great western plains were conquered on wheels. The heartland was reached by navigable rivers. To the south, because of the very exuberance of the tropical jungle which grows back with incredible speed to swallow roadbeds built by man at tremendous costs, and because of the necessity of climbing the gigantic Andes by extraordinary feats of engineering to carry civilization to the highland valleys—whether by sixteenth century roads or twentieth century railroads and highways—our struggle with geography has been and still is heroic.

On account of these hardships that nature has put in our way, we have built a civilization that demanded a far greater effort than yours. Twenty independent progressive nations are proof of our firm determination to succeed. The powerful European nations with vast resources at their disposal, under similar conditions, in some cases on our own continent, have failed to achieve the degree of development that we have. France first and the United States later sampled the great difficulties of construction in the tropics in building the Panama Canal.

Not only has geography favored the northern part of the hemisphere, geology as well has been generous to your part of the world. Although the southern part of the hemisphere is rich in mineral resources, nowhere else can be found the immense deposits of iron ore, almost inexhaustible coal mines, and rich oil fields which are practically underneath your cities and which constitute genuine miracles of nature. In our case our underground resources have not been so easily reached and some are so remotely located that they have not been exploited even today. We have attained maturity in a hard and painful way.

These are the main differences and there are many others, yet there are fewer differences than those that separate the countries of Europe, of Asia, or of Africa. Our countries have the same geographical and historical background. Although it would be a mistake to make sweeping statements about the continent, we would be in no danger to say that all people, whether white or brown or black or shades thereof, hope for a life of prosperity, social justice, and freedom. Hence, generalization when talking of the possibility of democracy in Latin America is not, by any means, an absurdity.

The twentieth century has brought about great changes both in North and South America, changes which have probably contributed to bringing the two people closer together and reducing the proportion of the differences in their backgrounds. The same indomitable spirit of the pioneers that pushed the covered wagons across the great plains to the shores of the Pacific is evident during the twentieth century in your tremendous capacity for constructive action and remarkable genius for invention. Thanks to your wise political and economic structure you became the great industrial country that you are today.

In South America the tremendous drawbacks of political instability and geographical barriers to economic advancement were partially offset in the last few decades by rational exploitation of natural resources, the building of roads, the use of the airplane, and the great advancement in medicine which made possible the protection of human lives under the most adverse climatic conditions. The continued struggle of the common man to see his dream of liberty and justice and material well-being come true has helped improve working conditions, made education available to the masses, and brought about, undoubtedly, changes for the better that have translated themselves into a remarkable economic revival.

Although much still has to be done for the well-being of the masses, Latin America is no longer the remote uncivilized frontier. Her cities are no longer pestholes reeking with bubonic plague and yellow fever. The airliner and modern highways are bringing into production new, rich, unexploited land; great cities have grown at a much faster rate than those of the United States. Industrial development, particularly during the last decade, has contributed toward improving the standard of living of the people. The battle against malaria, yellow fever, small pox, yaws, and other Biblical scourges is already won; heretofore unknown figures of population increases are appearing. One cannot imagine what new horizons science will open in regions like the Amazon valley, for instance, that immense tract of land that has hardly been scratched by man.

We have seen how fast the North had grown from a few scattered English colonies and how the South had remained stagnant, but now, in the twentieth century, again the population of Latin America exceeds that of the United States, growing at a faster rate than any other continent. The index of growth of population in Latin America is 1.9 per cent, while that of the U. S. is 1.4 per cent (UN *Demographic Yearbook*). In 1950 the population was 150,697,361 for the United States and 152,800,000 for Latin America.

What has been the political picture during this century? Anyone over forty years of age in the United States and elsewhere was born in the horse and buggy age. All the great inventions and modern conveniences that are taken as a matter of fact by the younger generations came about during our lifetime. During the last forty years the world has experienced the two most destructive wars in the history of humanity; we have been witnesses to the disappearance of all absolute monarchies in the civilized world. New political ideologies that for a moment seemed on the road to success have come and gone with their leaders, and a new menace, communism, has grown from the backrooms of exiles and discontented dreamers in London, Paris, Switzerland, and the underground in Russia to such gigantic proportions that it dominates half the world and constitutes today the greatest menace to our way of life. Our generation, the world over, has seen more changes than fifty generations before us, and you Americans, in particular, have lived and experienced in a few years more drastic and spectacular change than has been the fortune or misfortune of any people in the past.

Not so many years ago, your great nation, protected from the political turmoils in the rest of the world by two great ocean barriers, and with a heritage of a subcontinent that still had frontiers to conquer, was living a life of abundance within your great tradition of freedom, tolerance, and democratic government. Then, one day, not more than thirty years ago, a young American, a typical product of his environment, flew the Atlantic non-stop in a small plane. Your great ocean barriers became avenues of approach. The most distant points on earth became only hours away, and your country found itself vulnerable to attack from without. Your sense of security that up to then had been a part of your make-up, taken as a matter of fact, was suddenly shattered. From that day on your outlook on life had to change. Your political policies, both national and international, became obsolete. From that day on the United States had to concern herself with the rest of the world as a matter of self-preservation. When the second World War was fought and the United States emerged from the smoke of battle as the new leader of the world, she found her leadership challenged by a powerful nation and its allies, nations which not only had great weapons of destruction at their command, but a new philosophy of life which needs for survival and success the liquidation of our own Christian civilization.

This has been the experience of this generation of Americans. One must admit that from the horse and buggy age to the dawn of the atomic era there have been tremendous changes that call for drastic readjustments. Values have changed, solid traditions have disappeared, and not always have the human brain and the human heart been able to keep up with the swiftness of the change. The changing scene during the twentieth century has not been as drastic for us in Latin America as it has been for you. Of course, we have lived through all the material advancements that have been the wonders of this age, but in our international political life we have been more witnesses than actors. As many nations loosely linked we have not had to carry the great responsibilities that you have as new leaders of the civilized world.

On the other hand, our nations have always been interdependent among themselves and with other nations of the world. We were never as self-integrating as the United States has been in the past. We have a long tradition of international relations; we are not new at the game as you are, a fact that might come in handy during these trying times in which fundamental matters for both of us are at stake.

Not much can be achieved in improving the relations between North and South Americans without an understanding of the cultural and psychological characteristics of the people. All true understanding does not emanate from government policy, it must come from the people; therefore, a real comprehension of the mutual problems and complexities of the respective cultures and psychological make-up is indispensable.

In order to visualize more clearly the difference in psychology and temperament, let us examine two extreme impressions which represent by no means the average views, but unfortunately many eyes both in the North and in the South visualize their neighbors through impressions based, in most cases, on half truths. The extreme North American view of Latin America is that of a vast tropical, exotic land, covered with palm trees, with immense undeveloped natural resources that are awaiting Yankee energy and ingenuity to be properly exploited for his benefit exclusively, a land inhabited by a docile, colorful, and shiftless people of an inferior mongrel race who sit around dreaming in an abstract, humanistic, and idealistic spiritual world with an olympic disregard for the better material things of life. The extremist, in this case, sees only one future for Latin America: U. S. capital and know-how combined with cheap labor should exploit efficiently untold natural resources as a means of achieving still greater prosperity for the people of the United States, in short, economic colonialism. If the plan for some reason should not work, why not shift American capital and efforts to Asia and Africa where labor might be cheaper still.

On the other hand, the extreme Latin American picture of his North American neighbor is that he is the logical product of racial prejudice, extreme nationalism, and a materialistic pragmatic philosophy, who, although having at his disposal mechanical means for an extraordinarily comfortable existence, is incapable of enjoying the more lasting values of the intellect. He is supposed to be a barbarian, well-intentioned, highly specialized, but immature mentally; he is trying to impose his utilitarian materialistic culture upon a people that look at life from the lofty pedestal of a higher and more spiritual realm. The extremist from the South sees only one imminent and urgent course of action: take every step to defend his higher culture and intellectual values from the invasion of a materialistic, however comfortable, interpretation of life.

Of course, these are two extreme views put forth in terms of exaggeration and simplification of concepts, but they serve to point out the real existence of differences in point of view, psychological make-up, and cultural background between the people of the North and the South. We are more idealistic by nature, while you are realistic; we are individualists, while you are more capable of collective enterprise.

Fortunately, realities of today are contributing more than anything to minimize gradually all differences. Now that the North American has created a great industrialized nation that has made it possible to bring about a higher standard of material well-being, there is a healthy trend towards recognition of the values of the spirit which will eventually lead to a greater and deeper enjoyment of life. On the other hand, Latin America has realized that it is impossible to live in a dream world in the twentieth century and that she must learn much from her neighbors to the north to convert her resources and potentialities into a higher standard of living for the masses. In this field, there can be a meeting of the minds and an exchange of valuable contributions which can be of tremendous benefit to both cultures and bring them closer together than they have ever been in the past, without, on the other hand, losing any of the basic elements of their respective cultures.

After this brief analysis of the differences and analogies in the value system and point of view between Latin Americans and North Americans, we can draw the following conclusions:

1. No other group of nations in the world have more similarities and ties among them, in spite of their differences, than the countries of Latin America.

2. Considering the differences and similarities between Latin Americans and North Americans, the simi-

larities far outweigh the differences. We are closer to North Americans in our newer and more hopeful conception of life. We more and more look upon each other as neighbors, inhabitants of the New World, and no longer have our eyes set on Europe alone.

3. Lastly, our destiny is one of interdependence and integration. North Americans are becoming more world-minded, more humanistic, while Latin Americans are becoming more pragmatic, more specialized. We are all striving to obtain the benefit of team work within the continent, utilizing our own human and natural resources. It can be said without exaggeration that we are now looking upon the birth of a new type of human being, the man of the New World, the master of a new era, the dawn of which we are now contemplating.

CHAPTER II

ECUADOR—AN EXPERIMENT IN DEMOCRACY

THE EXPERIMENT IN democracy which I will try to describe took place in a typical Latin American country. There are cities within its boundaries that have climates equivalent to those of all the cities of the continent. At different altitudes above sea level all known crops can be grown; consequently, all the problems of production to be found anywhere in the hemisphere are here. The country is not the poorest, nor is it among the richest; it is not the most European in culture, nor is it the most modern. It is one of the most Latin American; in short, Ecuador is a cross-section of the realities of the continent.

The people are good and hard-working to a degree of intensity that in some cases borders on desperation when the barest necessities of life have to be hoed out of a steep slope of the Andes, ten thousand feet above the sea. They possess ancient virtues that have not been lost, possibly because of a slow rhythm of progress; they are hospitable, patient, and have an extraordinary ability for handicraft. The old churches in Quito, gems of colonial baroque architecture with their magnificent paintings, sculptures, and wood carvings, established this city, where the first art school was founded by the

AN EXPERIMENT IN DEMOCRACY

Franciscan monks in 1533, as the cradle of art in the Western Hemisphere. This noble artistic heritage has not been lost.

The people have a long-standing tradition of love for freedom, ever present throughout the history of the nation, from the revolt against taxation by the Spanish king in the seventeenth century, through the heroic Wars of Independence, to the permanent struggle for liberty throughout the convulsive history of the republic. The people of Ecuador have never tolerated despotism for long, nor have they ever exchanged freedom for bread.

To understand further the people we must take a look at the country. It is one of the Andean countries on the Pacific Ocean, exactly in the middle of the world, crossed by the equatorial line at latitude zero degrees, and bordered by Colombia to the north and Peru to the south. Its size, some 116,000 square miles, is about the equivalent of Italy. Three and a half million people inhabit the country. Nine Latin American countries are larger than Ecuador, ten smaller; seven have a larger population, twelve a smaller. The surface of Ecuador may be divided into three different regions. The coastal plain, covered by some of the richest volcanic soil to be found anywhere in the world, extends from the Andean foothills to the Pacific Ocean. It is traversed by the Guayas, the largest navigable river from Oregon to Patagonia. The inter-Andean region, a high plateau between two lofty mountain chains which cross the republic from north to south, between and about parallel to the 78th and 79th meridians, is divided into valleys by transversal mountain ranges, as the steps in a ladder. The mean elevation of these valleys is about 8,400 feet above sea level. To the east and west, around the central plain, arise twenty-two snow-clad peaks, some active volcanos. Among them is Cotopaxi, more than 19,000 feet above sea level, the highest active volcano in the world. Nowhere else can be found such an impressive sight, a great avenue lined by snow-clad peaks between 15,000 and 21,000 feet above the sea in apparent symmetrical arrangement in parallel lines, sometimes in pairs, facing each other across the Cyclopean passage. The third region is the Oriente, a great forest-covered plain descending from the high mountains towards the east, interlaced by a network of large rivers flowing into the Amazon. This is the part of the upper Amazon basin occupied also by Colombia, Peru, and Brazil. This region is considered as a reserve for future expansion. Finally, there are the legendary Galápagos Islands, six hundred miles from the mainland, where the theory of evolution was born at the time Charles Darwin visited the Islands in 1835. A geographic institute, in which all the continent is interested, will soon continue investigations of a scientific nature in this region which is unique with primitive characteristics nowhere duplicated on earth.

Climatic conditions in Ecuador are very largely contingent on altitude. Contrary to what might be expected, the climate is not torrid on the coast and frigid in the high valleys. The cold Humboldt Current which sweeps up the west coast of South America from the Antarctic Ocean has a moderating influence on the climate. The influence of this cold current is extraordinary. While in Chile and Peru to the south it has affected the climate to a degree that has rendered the coastal plain completely barren, without a drop of rainfall whatsoever, and beyond the northern boundary of Ecuador as the current turns at right angles and flows west away from the continent, the lowlands are a teeming jungle, in Ecuador the coast is green and the weather mild, and up in the highlands clear skies and radiant sunshine make it easier for man to live in higher altitudes than anywhere else on earth. Ecuador, thus, has every range of temperature, from the tropics to eternal snows. There are two seasons, wet and dry. During the wet season it usually rains in the afternoons or at night and the mornings are full of sunshine. The dry season is broken up now and then by an occasional shower. This extraordinary range of climatic conditions permits the cultivation of temperate zone crops in the high inter-Andean valleys, which are consumed within the country, while the fertile soils of the coast produce cocoa, coffee, rice, and bananas. These crops, plus many others in lesser quantities, are exported.

The population is made up of white, mestizo, and pure Indian elements, each composing about one third of the country's total human resources. However, this would be only a numerical proportion and by no means would it be equally balanced in the economic and cultural assets of these three parts. There is an ever-increasing migration from the densely populated, overfarmed inter-Andean valleys to the rich, uncultivated lowlands. The Amazon region is scarcely populated and there still can be found savage Indians, among them the famous head hunters.

An interesting fact is that while in most countries the land of the future, the frontier, so to speak, is always remote and difficult to reach, in Ecuador it is to be found at the foot of the Andes, close to the ocean and covered by rich volcanic ash, comparable in fertility only to the soil found in the island of Java, as an American scientist once pointed out. Ecuador is a country of many cities and towns, at different altitudes with a great variation in climate; we do not have the problem of the great metropolis that absorbs most of the urban population. The largest cities are Quito, the capital, with 250,000 inhabitants, and Guayaquil, the main port, with 320,000. There are some ten towns with a population ranging from 18,000 to 60,000. About 70 per cent of the population is rural, which is an important stabilizing factor and ensures a large labor force for agricultural production. According to the 1950 census there is an illiterate population of 42 per cent, which is not, by far, the worst in Latin America. The government is that of a centralized republic, where powers are defined by a written constitution. The chief organs are an executive

AN EXPERIMENT IN DEMOCRACY

consisting of a president and vice president; a national congress consisting of two houses, a senate and a chamber of deputies; the judiciary; and the electoral function, which operates through a set of autonomous tribunals and boards for the supervision of elections.

Now a few words on Ecuadoran history as a background. At the time of the Spanish conquest, Ecuador was part of the great Inca empire that included what is today Ecuador, Peru, Bolivia, and northern Argentina. Not many years before the arrival of the Spanish invaders, war broke out between the brothers Huascar and Atahualpa between whom their father, the great Inca Guaynacapac, had divided the empire. Atahualpa and his legions from Quito decisively defeated the forces of Huascar from Cuzco. The Spanish invader took advantage of the state of confusion and weakness after the great internal struggle, and without too much trouble captured Atahualpa and put him to death. The fact that Atahualpa was an absolute monarch in a political system that completely disregarded the will of the people brought about the complete collapse and total disintegration of his empire the minute he disappeared from the scene.

Towards the close of the eighteenth century the desire for independence began to manifest itself throughout the Spanish colonies of Latin America. The first attempt to overthrow the Spanish yoke in South America was made in Quito in 1809 and bloodily suppressed by the Spanish king. Only with the help of the great liberator, Simón Bolívar, was the country freed in 1822, and it became for eight years, with Colombia and Venezuela, part of the triple confederation called Grand Colombia. In 1830 Bolívar's dream of a great nation disintegrated to become what today are the independent republics of Colombia, Ecuador, Venezuela and Panama.

Our history as an independent republic can be divided roughly into four different periods. The first was an era of military dictators, with the title of president, dominated by the generals of the Wars of Independence and their heirs, who fought among themselves for political power. One enlightened statesman appeared on the scene during this period and left the seed of liberty, but soon was engulfed by reactionaries. The second period was mainly dominated by the Conservative party, but especially by a sector with a unique theocratic conception of the state, which, instead of maintaining religion within the high spiritual fields where it belongs, tried to use it as a tool for politics and to satisfy the greed for power. A revival of liberalism followed when the only real revolution, in 1895, brought about drastic political reforms, highlighted by the separation of church and state. During the following years a trend away from military intervention in the affairs of state was leading towards stable government, but was interrupted in 1925 when native politics in several countries became contaminated by the examples of the totalitarian movements in Italy and Germany. The new political

AN EXPERIMENT IN DEMOCRACY

order proposed to solve all the country's problems by putting it into a political strait jacket, but only succeeded in starting an era of chaos. This period was interrupted by a few tries at constructive government, only to sink back into chaos again.

If in the past, from 1830 to 1895, the fact that the country had eleven constitutions was proof of our instability, during the twenty-three years up to 1947 all previous records were broken. In this short period of time Ecuador had twenty-seven chiefs of state, four presidents in one month, six constitutions, and innumerable so-called revolutions, many of which failed while others were successful. These twenty-three years of chaos all but destroyed democracy. Barracks revolts and electoral frauds changed governments; political opponents were imprisoned or banished from the country. Men, women, and children lost their lives in useless clashes of arms between factions, hate was undermining the nation, and all moral and spiritual values were decadent. The country as a whole came to a standstill. No one party or ideology was responsible for the victims of the situation. All were responsible and suffered the consequences. Chaos had swallowed them all. As a result of this political and social disorder the people lost all hope, looked with disbelief upon any civic activity, and the destiny of the republic fell into the hands of a few, some too impractical, others too ambitious, but in no case were they representative of the people. The Ecuadoran people had seldom been responsible for their governments, which in most cases came to office by fraud or force, so it was only logical that the people considered these governments as something distant and remote and could do no more than deplore them.

But slowly the masses became aware of the tragic road their country was following. They came to realize their responsibilities and concluded it was high time to take their destiny into their own hands. This is how in 1947 a military dictator who had overthrown the government was overthrown himself by the force of public opinion in a week's time. Then congress convened to elect a president who, with a deep sense of responsibility and with the backing of the whole country, presided over the free and unadulterated elections in which I was elected.

What was the political map of the country at the time of my election? All three major political parties were dated in their approach to realities of the times. The Conservative party, with a large backing of landowners and peasants in the highlands, still insisted on bringing the Catholic Church into the political picture and using the Church's prestige and spiritual strength for its own designs. The Liberal party, with the coast as its stronghold, which had been in power for forty-five years maintained the same anti-clerical position that had made it possible to segregate church and state and introduce major political reforms after 1895. Anti-clericalism obviously could not be maintained as a major issue fifty years later, when problems of a social nature were paramount in all political thinking. This party, which had been revolutionary and progressive at the time of the 1895 revolution, slowly lost its momentum and prestige through its long stay in power until today it finds itself, as during the past few years, about on a par with the Conservatives in matters of social programs. The Socialist party does not seem to realize that the great ideological cleavage between democracy and communism lies to the left of it, and carries on in a state of great confusion, with the true socialists outside of the party and those within following the Communist party line to the letter. A few genuine leaders have tried to guide the party back to its true course and have been expelled for their efforts by Marxist directors that have pulled the wool over the eyes of their followers among workers and students. The Communist party, although well organized, is among the smaller political groups. With these shortcomings many Ecuadorans refused to follow any of the traditional parties and planned a new, up-to-date, realistic, thoroughly Ecuadoran political and social program which attracted a majority of citizens from all walks of life, from the landowners to the workers, and which, under the name of National Civic Democratic Movement, elected me.

This was the country of which I became president in 1948. My background was quite different from that of the typical chief of state of the past. My previous experiences in public life had been at the municipal level as mayor of the city of Quito, in close contact with problems of national government as minister of national defense, and at the international level as ambassador to Washington. This background might suggest a continued and active interest in politics; in fact, the truth was quite the opposite. I was not a politician and had no illusions about the game that so fascinates some. I had been more of a spectator than an actor in politics. I had led an active, practical life in close contact with the soil, wrestling with the problems of production, as a farmer in the highlands. This type of experience gave me a new point of view which made possible a fresh approach to the task of government and that was precisely what my compatriots wanted and needed.

Ingrained deeply in my make-up I had the teachings and the examples of my father, a champion of liberalism and of democratic ideas, who, as president, had introduced drastic political reforms and governed with a deep sense of respect for democracy. On the other hand, as a student in the United States I had learned to admire the American way of life, which led me to start another experiment in democracy on a smaller scale—the founding of the American School of Quito, an unusual institution, with faculty half American and half Ecuadoran, some subjects taught in Spanish and others in English in an atmosphere of true democracy with the hope of inspiring a new generation with a better understanding of our two cultures.

When I took office in 1948 I realized the situation called for drastic changes. If so many of my predecessors had failed and been overthrown, why follow the political formulas that had been responsible for their undoing? I put my ear to the ground and listened to what the people for a long time had been saying and hoping in vain, and made up my mind to act according to their wishes. My first words were a message of freedom, of respect for the will of the people, of strict obedience to the law. I did not promise miracles overnight; the country would not be done over in a flash. I promised hard work to set the foundations for future prosperity. I asked all my countrymen to join in the task, and to become actors, not spectators, in building a nation. I spoke of social justice, of better times, and of opportunities for work that would bring about higher standards of living in an atmosphere of peace and liberty and justice. I finally promised them that from that date on I was not only the president of those who had elected me, but of all the Ecuadorans. The people believed this simple message, inspired in the principles of democracy, because they had a deep yearning for freedom and peace.

With the solid backing of the people my experiment in democracy in its truest and purest manifestation started. It was what the people wanted. I had faith in them and a deep conviction concerning democracy and the possibility of making it work successfully in a Latin American country. I believed that the long and painful road of mistakes and errors had made the people capable of distinguishing what they did not want from what they should have, if they were only given a chance to live under the principles of democracy. I realized that the strength I had, the only strength I wanted and needed, resided in the people. When the government started operating in 1948, within the strict limits set by democratic principles, absolute liberty of speech, deepest respect for the constitution and laws of the republic, and an atmosphere of peace and security and respect for human dignity were created.

The country had to make up for valuable lost time. Much had to be done for the economic development that would bring about a better standard of living for the people. It would have been much easier and more expedient to act with no concern for the limitations of democratic government or the criticism of public opinion, but at what cost—perhaps great and swift material accomplishments in exchange for still greater and deeper spiritual sacrifices. To govern democratically is to do it the hard way; it takes longer to accomplish things, but progress is steadier and of a more solid nature; it is what the people want after they have had a chance to decide *what* they want.

It was not necessary for me, as it is in the case of dictators, to embark on hastily planned programs of public works with an eye on personal prestige rather than on permanent beneficial results for the country. My government took a long view in plans for the prog-

AN EXPERIMENT IN DEMOCRACY 33

ress and modernization of the sources of production. Much of what has been done will only bear significant fruit long after my term in office, though the efficiency in planning is already evident in the steadily improving volume of production and notable increase in varieties of export.

From the very start of my term I sought the aid of scientific and technical knowledge from many sources: the U. S. Government through the Institute of Inter-American Affairs and the Point Four Program; the Mexican Government (that helped us to study irrigation problems); the United Nations and its different organizations, such as the Food and Agriculture Organization, the United Nations International Children's Emergency Fund, the Office of International Trade, and the Economic Commission for Latin America; the Organization of American States; and private institutions, such as the International Basic Economy Corporation and the Kellogg Foundation. With this very valuable assistance from outside the country and our own sources of know-how, we were able to prepare over a hundred studies for economic development that constitute a blueprint for action.

In an atmosphere of political tranquility and according to preconceived plans much was accomplished. It was possible for the first time in the history of the country to make a complete census of the population in 1950. With the assistance of the World Health Organization, all Ecuadorans from twenty years of age were vaccinated against tuberculosis, complementing in this manner the splendid work carried out by the Ecuadoran Tuberculosis League, which has managed to cut in half the death rate from tuberculosis in thirteen years. A campaign against malaria, started in 1948, has managed to eliminate that energy-sapping disease as a major problem for the country. Roads and schools were built. A new major export crop, bananas, became over a period of no more than four years our largest item for export. The country grew faster economically during these four years, in spite of a major earthquake in 1949 and large floods in 1950, than it had ever grown in the past. The people of Ecuador had finally been able to get down to work, thanks to political stability.

Even matters of a superficial nature helped change the atmosphere about the government. Much of the formality that took up valuable time was done away with. The presentation of credentials by the representative of a foreign government, for instance, called for very elaborate procedures. The president and his cabinet, dressed in morning coats, would receive the envoy and formal speeches would be pronounced. This was changed to a simple ceremony in which the president and minister of foreign affairs alone, without the rest of the cabinet, which was not distracted from more important chores, would receive the envoy; the speeches would be exchanged in closed envelopes for reading later; and an informal, friendly interview would take place. The presidential guard had been up to then

AN EXPERIMENT IN DEMOCRACY

quite a substantial armed contingent. It was reduced to a few friendly, inconspicuous guards.

I made it a practice to receive all callers, from all walks of life, once a week. A typical day would witness a cross section of the country filing through the presidential office: a college professor, a distinguished visitor from abroad, a factory worker, a group of Indians from the highlands, a poor widow, and sometimes a crank.

I mingled with the crowds at sports events, walked the street accompanied only by my aide, and on week ends drove my station wagon to the country with my wife and children. During my four years in office I lived in my own modest home. My intention was to do away with all the expensive trappings that should have no place in an American democratic country. I think the president should always be in close contact with his people, not a remote, feared demi-god, but an approachable, understanding human being. Tradition went out the window to the extent that the long-established habit of a full-course, midday dinner, sometimes topped off by a corresponding siesta, which took up about three hours daily, was eliminated and the president substituted for it a sandwich and a glass of milk at his desk. My efforts to humanize the office of president paid off in the way the people responded in terms of friendship, respect, and confidence.

During the 1950 census a community of culturally remote Indians refused to cooperate with the census, and several dangerous uprisings took place. Local authorities and enumerators were attacked and in some cases barely managed to escape with their lives. I flew to the scene of the difficulty and spoke to the Indians, explaining in a friendly manner what the census meant in order to dissipate their fears. They finally agreed to submit to the census on the condition that I remain among them during the enumeration, and we had no further troubles.

Many old-time politicians and men of experience questioned the soundness of these new methods of government. The members of my own cabinet had a long and confidential meeting with me; they were honestly concerned with the danger of being misunderstood by a people whom they considered were not ready to assume all the responsibilities involved in self-government. They recommended a gradual process that would slowly reach the stage of action that I had already put into effect. The sincerity and conviction with which I tried to convince my friends and collaborators won them over, and I am glad to state that their devotion to the cause was a powerful reason for its success.

The Ecuadoran people found themselves, for the first time in history, enjoying a peaceful, free and protected existence that was the immediate result of stable, truly representative government. A few, very few, abused their privileges, particularly in connection with freedom of the press. I was attacked with unprecedented baseness by almost hysterical political detractors. None of my predecessors had ever suffered or would

AN EXPERIMENT IN DEMOCRACY

have tolerated the degree of vilification without once retaliating by word or deed. My tolerance encouraged abuse at first, but the outcome was that public opinion in the country turned its back on all outbreaks of false and unjust abuse which appeared in a minor but virulent sector of the press. The great majority of the press realized that freedom had certain moral limitations and accordingly played, with a deep sense of responsibility, the very important role that a free press must necessarily have in a democracy.

My predecessors as presidents, all patriotic and well-meaning, usually found themselves dedicating their time, energies, and talents to keeping from being overthrown, and their plans for constructive action had to be postponed in favor of the necessity for survival. This was not my experience. There was no necessity to waste time in petty politics to keep from falling off the presidential tightrope. The backing of the people made it possible for the government to walk always on solid ground.

The armed forces, which in the past had many times been the instrument for oppression of the people, adopted a new, responsible, and patriotic attitude that contributed more than anything else in stabilizing the institution of government. In 1947 the army had already intervened to save the country from falling into one of the usual illegal governments which she had suffered many times in the past. During my regime the armed forces had the opportunity to prove that they were no longer straying away from the straight and narrow path of defense of their country and its constitution. Once in Quito, in 1949, a group of retired army officers tried to revive practices that had been successful in the past and attacked by surprise the barracks of an armored batallion in the outskirts of the city. They soon came in contact with a young lieutenant, who refused to listen to their promises, and the whole group was shortly arrested. Again, in Guayaquil in 1951, a group that had the support of most of the lower elements in the city, which had been terrorized by them for months, took over control of the municipal palace one night and broadcast the news to the rest of the country that the local garrison had surrendered to them; but as soon as they came in contact with the first army men, they were promptly overpowered and put in jail. The army's attitude, which has served to gain for them great prestige, seems to have ended forever in our country the old military coup which was, and unfortunately still is in some countries, typical of the so-called Latin American revolution.

Many pointed to the fact that normal constitutional government could not possibly cope efficiently with situations of emergency, which necessarily would call for swift and drastic action impossible under the limitations of democratic government. A vivid example of how effective lawful government can be is the dramatic accomplishment in the increase in production and export of bananas during a four-year period without once overstepping the rigid limits of the law. Ecuador's major export crop during the war had been rice, but in 1947 the price of rice in the world markets started such a rapid decline that by 1948 world prices were lower than costs of production in Ecuador. Ecuador needed badly a new export crop to replace the fast-fading rice crop.

One day in 1948 I was visited in my office by some high officials of United Fruit who had been inspecting their plantations on the coast of Ecuador. At that time most of the large plantations in Central America had been practically destroyed by Panama disease and I had asked, with great interest, whether the United Fruit men had found any indications of Panama disease in Ecuador. They said they had not, but that even if the disease appeared in the very near future, Ecuador would still have ten good years of banana production. This bit of technical advice put the government to work encouraging planting of bananas, particularly through special credits for banana growing through the National Development Bank. The proof of how efficiently the government had planned the increase in production of this new export crop is in the following figures: in 1948 Ecuador exported a little less than two million dollars in bananas; in 1952 she exported over twenty million dollars in bananas and became the world's largest exporter. The limitations of representative lawful government did not in any way interfere with the successful planning of a major economic emergency problem.

There also was another opportunity to put the experiment to a still greater test under the most trying and extraordinary circumstances. My country was the victim, in 1949, of one of the most destructive earthquakes in the world during the last decade; 6,000 people were killed and over 100,000 were left homeless, by official International Red Cross count, and the damage was calculated at a hundred million dollars. The following year a flood put our most important railroad, the most vital connection between the highland and the sea, out of service for ninety days. Another flood caused severe damage to Cuenca, the third largest city in the country. Our main export crop during the war years, rice, was a victim of falling quotations in a world market that was readjusting to normal. All these were major problems of a staggering importance for a small and poor country, but the government did not use the situation as an excuse to ask for extraordinary powers from congress, which it could have under the constitution, because it would have meant curtailing liberties and depriving the people of their newly granted rights. The constitution and laws of the country proved ample and sufficient to meet the situation. Democracy showed it was just as effective in emergencies as it was in normal times.

At the end of four years the country had gained international respectability as she had never before enjoyed. In an atmosphere of liberty, peace, justice, and respect for human dignity, the Ecuadoran people were able to work and live and take a big step toward progress, as these few figures can prove. Export doubled during the 1948-1952 period in comparison with the four previous years. The Chase National Bank in its quarterly publication of September, 1953, reported that: "Ecuador showed greater trade progress than any other Latin American republic last year (1952). The reason: greatly increased crop output and exports. Value of total exports rose by an impressive 48%. Imports were up 20%."

A graph in the same publication indicates that the volume of farm exports is far above early postwar years. The percentage of increase during 1952 above the 1947-1949 average of the four major export crops was bananas 25 per cent, coffee 52 per cent, cacao 31 per cent and rice 10 per cent.

On August 31, 1952, for the first time in twenty-eight years, a president of Ecuador was able to complete his term of office and turn over the government to a successor who was freely elected by the people. The new president is not my political friend. There was a danger of many of my projects being thrown overboard, but he was the citizen chosen by a majority of the people. The lot of an ex-president is usually not a happy one in most cases in Latin America. Sometimes he does not escape with his life. In other instances he has to live in exile far from his country and in many cases he is simply forgotten. But this has not been my experience. The night I became again a plain citizen I was carried home on the shoulders of a crowd. My clothes were torn for souvenirs. To this day I cannot walk the streets in Quito or appear at public functions without receiving proof of the gratitude of my people.

This has been my experience; the experiment in democracy did not blow up in my face, as many feared. The formula is simple and here it is for all to follow— GIVE THE GOVERNMENT BACK TO THE PEOPLE!

CHAPTER III

DEMOCRACY IN LATIN AMERICA—
PAST AND FUTURE

WE HAVE LOOKED at the experiment in democratic government in Ecuador, supposedly a classic country in which to study all the chronic problems that plague many Latin American states: revolutions, militarism, and ineffectively written constitutions. We have also seen how a truly democratic government can blossom out, if given a chance, because the people are fundamentally democratic.

If we lift our sights from the particular case of Ecuador to the continent as a whole, we find the same characteristic: the people of Latin America are basically democratic. The fact that dictators have always had to rely on bayonets and prison chains as instruments of oppression in order to subsist is proof of the presence of opposing forces against which they must be constantly on guard. The very revolutions by which dictators are overthrown are further proof of the undeniable thirst for freedom of the people of Latin America. Revolutions against democratic government are always founded on demagogic fabrications, which many times take advantage of the weakness, corruption, or tolerance of a democratic regime. Whatever the forces that act against democracy, there are countries like Mexico,

Costa Rica, Ecuador, Uruguay, and Chile where a truly democratic spirit has been able to survive.

Mexico, the great nation to the south of the United States, your closest neighbor, is unique among Latin American nations in the fact that as no other, her people have created a distinct and typical culture based primarily on the historical background and the racial make-up of the population. Mexico in the past not only had to fight her war of independence from the mother country, as did the others, but she also had to fight for her existence against foreign invaders, not once, but several times. These experiences have given the Mexicans a deep-rooted awareness of nationality and love of freedom, many times defended at the cost of their blood. Furthermore, Mexico underwent vast and swift social, political, and economic change which was brought about by the revolution that started in 1910 with the overthrow of a dictatorship of long standing. This revolution, one of the very few real revolutions in Latin America since the Wars of Independence, affected the position of the church, the landholding system, the conditions of the lower classes, and the role of foreign capital. It contributed more than anything else toward the creation of a peculiar culture which is typically Mexican. This made itself evident in the political system in terms of a deep-rooted democratic way of government, which is responsible for political stability, internal peace, and a new era of material prosperity.

Costa Rica, a bright light in Central America, is a

PAST AND FUTURE

small country that has the unusual distinction of having more school teachers than soldiers. It is an isle of democracy. While her neighbors have been the frequent victims of violence and despotism, her people have lived a quiet and constructive life under enlightened, freely elected governments that have maintained a deep respect for human dignity and freedom. By all standards she is not an economic or political power in Latin America, but her voice carries far and is respected because of its great spiritual value.

Chile has a working democracy. With the development of industry and the economic movement from the fertile central valley to the arid nitrate fields and copper mines to the north during this century, a powerful industrial lower class appeared upon the scene as well as a strong urban middle class. This brought about a shifting of power downward in the social scale, which, coupled with the spread of formal education and the strong influence of an expanding free, daily press, has served to establish a deep-rooted democracy in the masses.

In Uruguay, democratic conviction is such that any kind of oppression is rejected to a point that foreigners find it difficult to understand and must adapt themselves to the peculiar Uruguayan conception of freedom, particularly if they come from countries where oppression and dictatorships are rampant. In Uruguay, liberty is an ingrained characteristic of the government, the legislators, the journalists, the workers, and the businessmen. A high living standard coupled with a high level of culture, thanks to a well-planned educational system, plus fifty years of stable, liberal government have created a healthy and tolerant middle class, which has helped make Uruguay a sanctuary for persecuted Europeans. Uruguay is a nation of peaceful people who have such a deep sense of institutional organization that they have constitutionally eliminated the office of president of the republic and put the executive power in the hands of a body of nine members, six elected from the majority party and three from the largest opposition party. This system assures a stable government as the principal issues are handled by parliament, a typical Uruguayan institution that really governs the country within the strictest legal limitations. However, the country would benefit by efficient modernization of her system of administration.

In other countries there is a long-standing tradition of democracy, deep in the conscience of the people, as in the case of Colombia. This country had one of the strongest and oldest democratic traditions in Latin America until a reactionary government in 1950 suppressed all civil rights and tried to put the country into a political strait jacket. This government, with a strong affinity to the Spanish dictatorship, was not tolerated for long by the freedom-loving Colombians, who, with the aid of the armed forces which had a proud record of never before intervening in politics, overthrew the government in 1953. Now Colombia is making

PAST AND FUTURE

rapid strides, in an atmosphere of tolerance and pacification, toward normalcy.

The people of Cuba are genuinely democratic; even dictators have not dared to interfere with freedom of the press. Haiti has always been a champion for human rights at all international conferences. The more enlightened classes have a deep sense of their country's remarkable destiny, not only in America, but in relation with the evolution towards democracy in other regions of the world. Her difficulties, as is the case in many other countries, are of an economic, health, and cultural nature. No other country has taken better advantage of international action for the improvement of the standard of living as a necessary requirement for true democracy than Haiti.

The Brazilians are liberal and tolerant by nature. Even when Brazil was an empire, from 1840 to 1889 the emperor, an enlightened, highly civilized man, was probably the greatest liberal and democrat of his time. This fact helped mould a peculiar type of mild dictatorship that can be found in the history of Brazil alone, and which is evolving today into a democracy with one of the most remarkable leaders Latin America has ever known. Brazil, larger in size than the United States, is the great land of the future. Her tremendous wealth and natural resources, hardly tapped at the present time, could maintain five times as many inhabitants as it does today. She can no doubt become in the not too distant future a power to be reckoned with. Although in the past she has shown little interest in affairs of the continent as a whole, she is becoming more and more hemispheric-minded as she realizes the important role that her future greatness has destined for her. A peace-loving, tolerant people in the process of creating a new race of men with a culture and a way of life all their own, with a rich and unexploited subcontinent at their command, Brazil is bound to play a decisive part in the future which will have a deep effect on the social and political structure of all Latin America and a growing influence in world affairs.

The speech delivered at the Tenth Inter-American Conference of Caracas,[1] in March, 1954, by Dr. Vicente Rao, Minister of Foreign Relations of Brazil, already shows this trend. He speaks for all of Latin America, rather than for Brazil alone, when he says:

"Speaking frankly, I must say that although we have obtained notable accomplishments in the political and juridical fields that have served to consolidate the spirit of Americanism which has united us all in a great body of nations, in the field of economic relations what has been done is very little or almost nothing, in proportion to what can be done and ought to be done.

". . . I will not attempt to comment on the pro-

[1] The Tenth International Conference of American States. These conferences are large diplomatic gatherings, which generally meet at five-year intervals and formulate basic agreements of Pan American policy. The first such meeting of representatives of the twenty-one independent republics took place in 1889, in Washington, the latest at Caracas in 1954.

found spirit of Americanism that inspired the important document, the Economic Charter of the Americas. But I cannot fail to recognize, if I must be frank, the lack of implementation of those provisions, nor would it be correct if I hid my justified fears as to the consequences of the weakening of economic cooperation among the sister nations of America.

"If we do not enforce the social-economic provisions of our Charter, if we fail to organize solidly the basis of our economic structure and consequently our social structure, and if we fail to raise the standard of living of our people to a level of human dignity, we will remain weak nations and such nations are the breeding grounds for the infectious germs of subversive ideologies, of the forces of disintegration which might destroy our Christian way of life, our free institutions, our independence and our sovereignty.

"We are all aware, Mr. President and gentlemen, that these germs and these forces of evil can only be subdued effectively when, in addition to weapons of another nature, they are attacked at their base, and this basic attack consists in effective elevation of the standard of living brought about by a solidly structured economic organization.

"I am well aware that private initiative and private capital, both domestic and foreign, were and still are great pioneers of progress and deserve protection and respect, when they are kept within the juridical and economic order of each country and within these limitations they cooperate towards development.

"But we all know, also, that neither private initiative nor private capital can alone solve all problems; none of us ignores, furthermore, that there are economic activities that must necessarily be carried out or controlled by the state, particularly in countries in the process of development, and these are activities that are the basis of the economic organization of a country.

"Commercial activities and industrial practices for profit are one thing, and another, quite different, is the basic organization of the economy that should be carried out at a higher level of economic policy, through investments made available in a spirit of cooperation under favorable conditions as to time and rate of interest, and in accordance with the possibilities of each nation, with an eye on the future and not on the immediate present.

"... Do difficulties stand in the way of this economic policy? No doubt, difficulties do exist and no one ignores them.

"... I ask, however, in spite of those problems and limitations, could we not put into effect, within reciprocal possibilities, something more real, more positive, more practical, than the eloquent and beautiful, but unimplemented, economic resolutions that we have up to now approved?

"... If this were done and by doing so we became strong, then we could proclaim *urbi et orbe* that not only is the continent capable of resisting all the assaults of the forces of evil, it is capable of defeating them and preserving with peace the civilization into which we were born and which was built with tremendous sacrifices by our forebears.

"If this were done we could rest assured that our political independence and our free institutions would prevail for our own welfare and that of humanity.

"But if we were not capable of doing so, it would be hopeless to entertain illusions, because grave and terrible would be the risks we must face in a weakened condition. And then the powerful countries as well as the weak, the so-called big and the small, all without exception, would be hurt by the consequences.

"Let us transform into something useful and effective our willingness to cooperate and complement economically. Let us proceed to adjust and fulfill our mutual needs—with an American spirit, with knowledge and understanding of our problems, of our virtues and of our shortcomings, with friendship and, above all, with good will."[2]

The credit side of the democratic balance sheet would not be complete without a brief reference to a new and different situation in two Latin American countries, Guatemala and Bolivia. Both have somewhat parallel past histories of despotic governments and a tremendous concentration of wealth in the hands of a few, in most cases foreign interests, which for reasons

[2] Translated by Galo Plaza and Alexander Heard from Inter-American Conference document 76 (Spanish), SP16, March 4, 1954. Original Portuguese.

of expediency have always preferred to deal with dictators. These two countries are undergoing a process of political and economic change. These changes may be the ingredients for a true revolution in the making that will improve the lot of the forgotten man. Many dangers are in sight in both cases, for one the inevitable errors that stem from inexperience in free government as well as dangers from the forces of reaction of the right, backed by the powerful interests that have lost or are losing their privileged situations. And from the left, what could be the greatest menace of them all, Communist infiltration, is growing, not so much because of the well-known tactics of international communism but because of the errors of those within and without the country who are playing into the very hands of communism by blindly refusing to recognize its presence and by refusing to admit the legitimate rights of the people to strive for a better standard of living under the guidance of their own governments. It must be stated that these dangers are present in different degrees in each of the two countries.

It is most interesting to quote some of the outstanding paragraphs of the speeches made at the Caracas Conference by the representatives of these two countries. These documents serve to point out the problems of a social-economic nature that are being faced in both countries. They indicate that communism in the Americas is trying to use for its own purpose what in many cases is a legitimate nationalistic aspiration and demonstrate the problems involved in fighting communism. We can see how here in America, as in other parts of the world, communism has managed to identify democracy with colonialism while she stands as a champion of nationalism, and how decisive it is in this great ideological struggle for the Western world to separate and clearly outline these issues.

This is what the Guatemalan Foreign Minister said at Caracas:

"The delegation of Guatemala is here, its head high, to express the legitimate aspirations of our people and the Revolutionary Government, solidly united in the desire and the effort to achieve an effective political and economic freedom, through the exercise of democracy, absolute respect for the political and social rights of man, and the development of an economic program in accordance with the present and future needs of the nation.

"The peoples of America followed with interest from the very beginning the events that have occurred in Guatemala since the heroic days of June and October 1944. Throughout its history Guatemala has been ravaged by enslaving regimes that had their origin in the colonial period and by brutal tyrannies of both Spanish and native origin, all of them predominantly feudal by nature. From the ruins of this tragic past, Guatemala has emerged with the unalterable determination to forge its own destiny without foreign interference, by means of a democratic system of government, in accordance with the vital needs of its people, respecting the rules of international law and motivated by the firm desire to maintain cordial relations with friendly countries and to comply faithfully with its international obligations.

"The policy of ransoming the national wealth and resources, neglected for entire decades, is motivated by nothing else than the wretchedness of our own people, resulting from the concentration of land and the backward structure of our economy. On the other hand, this policy conforms to the economic resolutions adopted by the United Nations and its specialized agencies, by the International Labor Organization, and by the Organization of American States with regard to economic development, agrarian reform, capital investment, social policy, and the exploitation of natural wealth and resources in behalf of the people.

"There is nothing novel or alien to the purposes of this Organization of American States in the program that is being carried out in behalf of the people of Guatemala. The whole policy of my Government is encompassed within the limits of representative democracy and has three great and fundamental objectives: growth of and absolute respect for democratic liberties; raising of the standard of living of the Guatemalan people through the transformation of a semi-feudal, semi-colonial economy into a capitalistic economy; and the defense of national sovereignty and independence.

"It is for this reason that in Guatemala freedoms

of expression of thought, of the press, of association, of labor organization, and of political organization, as well as the freedom to profess any religious creed, are not simply words contained in laws but tangible realities enjoyed to the full by the people. Guatemala is dedicated to the strengthening and the expansion of those freedoms and will not be a party, domestically or internationally, to any compromise that injures the rights of a single one of our compatriots.

"Our economic and social policy is based, fundamentally, on the following efforts:

"a. The humanization of labor-management relations in industrial and agricultural enterprises, through the enactment of organized labor laws that, far from provoking violent uprisings of workers made desperate by poverty, institutionalizes these labor-management relations within a system of basic social justice and administrative and judicial decisions in conformity with the law.

"b. The establishment of a social security system that covers only common accidents to workers, labor accidents, and a minimum maternal and child-care program, put into effect gradually and financed through the classic and conservative tripartite contribution from management, workers, and the State.

"c. The organization of a monetary and banking system adequate to meet credit and exchange needs and for the expansion and stability of our economy, in conformity with the most modern concepts of money and central banking originating in international agreements.

"d. The development of a broad domestic market through increases in the purchasing power and the elevation of the standard of living of the people, public investment, and the development of the rural economy, which up to now has been marginal and non-monetary.

"e. The liberation of the national economy through construction of means of communication to the ports and the producing zones; the construction of national docks; the development of an electrification plan adequate for industrial needs and for public consumption; and the subjection of foreign monopolistic enterprises to existing laws—on equal terms with domestic enterprise.

"f. The industrialization of the country through the organization of appropriate banking institutions and through an economic and legislative policy of industrial development followed by the State for the purpose of increasing the national income and domestic and foreign commerce.

"g. The liberation of the farmers through the abolition of semi-feudal and quasi-slave systems of work.

"The development of our agrarian economy through the redistribution of unproductive latifundia, furthering of land ownership in small holdings, the progressive increase of the sources of capital, and the organization of easy credit available to the farmers benefited by the democratic agrarian reform that has been carried out in the country by legal means since 1952.

". . . It would appear that all of these efforts, carried out with our own resources and with no assistance from without, would merit spiritual encouragement and moral aid . . . However, such has not been the case. 'Never in America has such a small country been subjected to such great pressure.'

". . . These bases and purposes of the Guatemalan revolution cannot be catalogued within a Communist ideology or policy: a political-economic platform like that put forward by the government of Guatemala, which is settling in rural areas thousands of individual landowners, individual farmers, can never be conceived of as a Communist plan. Far from that, we believe that raising the standard of living and the income of rural and urban workers alone stimulates the capitalistic economic development of the country and the sociological bases of a genuinely Guatemalan functional democracy.

". . . International reaction, at the same time it is pointing out Guatemala as a 'threat to continental solidarity,' is preparing vast interventionist plans, such as the one recently denounced by the Guatemalan government. The published documents—which the Department of State at Washington hastened to call Moscow propaganda—unquestionably show that the foreign conspirators and monopolistic interests that inspired and financed them sought to permit armed intervention against our country, as 'a noble undertaking against communism.' Let us emphasize before this Conference the gravity of these events. Non-intervention is one of the most priceless triumphs of Pan Americanism and the essential basis of inter-American unity, solidarity, and cooperation. It has been fully supported in various inter-American instruments, and specifically in Article 15 of the Charter of the Organization of American States. The Secretary General of the Organization, Dr. Alberto Lleras Camargo, in his report on the Ninth International Conference of American States, in commenting on this article, states categorically that with it 'the doubt that seemed to arise recently, as to whether intervention carried out collectively would be so considered, has thus been dispelled.' Subsequent to the Bogotá Conference, it has been alleged that 'Communism' is a good pretext to intervene collectively and to defeat the principle of non-intervention, and those interested have not failed to help in this defeat, regarding so-called 'communist infiltration' as a 'fifth column.' The same Secretary General of the Organization of American States, in the report mentioned, refutes this assumption and shows that there is absolutely no basis for it. Let me quote some of the ideas expressed by that authority. Mr. Lleras Camargo says: 'Who is the arbiter that can decide when intervention is just and is being conducted upon acceptable moral and juridical principles and when, on the contrary, it is pursuing imperialistic ends? The only judges would necessarily be the interested parties themselves, and every effective act of intervention by a world power would always find means of justification. In that way the most solid foundation of the freedom and independence of weak nations would be consumed in a single burnt offering to transitory circumstances, and the strong and imperialistic countries would have regained, with no effort, the most powerful of those arms of oppression that the progress of international law had wrenched from them.

" 'Obviously the effort to establish a distinction between collective and unilateral intervention, so as to justify the first and still condemn the second, was a dangerous flaw in the principle of non-intervention. The fact that a majority of nations within a given group combine to intervene in the internal affairs of a State by no means guarantees the goodness and uprightness of their purposes. No law apart from the individual or collective interest of the states would be applicable in that emergency. Today a group of democratic nations might combine to destroy, in a given country and by means of joint action and intervention, a form of antidemocratic government. But who is to guarantee that the coalition of a group of antidemocratic governments might not proceed in an identical manner against a government ruled by the most righteous laws and the most democratic institutions, if the only thing that makes the act legal is the fact that it is collective, that is, the number of parties that undertake intervention?'

"... If we ask ourselves what Pan Americanism has done for the peoples of America, and we want to be sincere in our reply, we shall have to admit that those peoples have often been deceived. Pan Americanism can do nothing for the effective benefit of man in America so long as it does not face the real problems of the hemisphere and the tremendous fact of a majority of nations with an underdeveloped economy, the peoples of which are prisoners of ignorance and poverty, in comparison with other highly industrialized nations, in relation to which they are kept in a semi-colonial dependent situation as suppliers of raw materials and cheap food, and as certain markets for their manufactured goods."[3]

There is no better way to discover the fears and hopes of Latin Americans and the problems that must be faced than to hear what their official spokesmen said at Caracas. Here are a few interesting paragraphs from the Bolivian representative:

"For the first time in half a century, the delegates to an Inter-American Conference are hearing the voice of the people of Bolivia.

"There are present here outstanding Americans who have known one another for many years, and who can recall the experiences of innumerable previous meetings, both of the Inter-American Conference itself, and of the specialized organizations. These men can bear

[3] Translated by Secretariat, Tenth Inter-American Conference document 95 (English), SP23, March 5, 1954. Original Spanish.

PAST AND FUTURE

witness to the fact that the voice raised by Bolivia at those meetings was almost imperceptible, even in its hours of greatest anguish, such as those of the Chaco War, or when my country was undergoing investigation by its sister nations of the hemisphere to determine whether or not, despite its small size and its weakness, it constituted a danger to America. The reason is that that feeble voice was not the voice of the people of Bolivia.

"The words, sometimes obsequious, sometimes boastful, but always weak and unsure, were those of lawyers for foreign corporations, diplomats ashamed of their nation of Indians and mestizos, and generals in the service of the oligarchy that sought to prevent the cries of the people from ever reaching the ears of the representatives of a free America.

"Meanwhile, the real people of Bolivia, composed of millions of Indians and mestizos, scattered in fields, workshops, factories, and mines, ignorant of, and ignored by, these meetings, were struggling in obscurity, but with tenacity, to win their right to life, well-being, and happiness.

". . . The National Revolution of Bolivia has, in the last two years, achieved greater gains than Bolivia was able to win in more than in a century of independence. Working conditions of the miners, whose average life span was 27 years, have been considerably improved, in spite of the limitations imposed by the actual prices of the minerals. Family and housing subsidies, a minimum wage, and collective labor contracts have been instituted.

"Lastly, free services, which were common in the feudal regime of the agricultural economy have been abolished.

". . . The problem of prices of raw materials affects us dramatically. We are a mineral-producing country, principally of tin. During the second world war we contributed to the defense of democracies with approximately 200 thousand tons of tin sold at controlled prices, which were disadvantageous from the point of view of Bolivia's economy. In that period, like others, we were urged to increase our production without sparing efforts and sacrifices, and this is naturally a difficult and costly proposition.

"It has happened more than once that, while we were producing at full capacity, the prices on the world market, over which we have no control, dropped vertically, with disastrous consequences.

"Not even in times of high quotations could we obtain the profits to which we felt we were entitled, because in such cases some way was always devised by which a ceiling price was imposed on tin, while no one cared to halt the drop in prices.

". . . The second world war proved that Bolivia is the only sure source of supply of tin for the defense of the free world in case of an emergency. For this reason it is desirable for all to have preferential treatment given to its production.

"Since the cooperation we receive is not sufficient for the accomplishment of our program of economic diversification, we are in need of new capital. Of course, we are interested in private capital; however, the hope that private capital investment can meet all our needs satisfactorily would only mean that we are wilfully deceiving ourselves.

"Private capital would have to come chiefly from the United States; however, the progress of technology in that country has opened new and vast possibilities to industry, particularly with respect to chemical products, which offer attractive returns to investors, and it is therefore unreasonable to hope that these investors would take the risk of investing in Latin America, toward which they have a long-standing and preconceived distrust.

"Moreover, the type of investment we need is exactly the kind that yields a low return; i.e., highway construction, hydroelectric works, and agricultural development.

"These are indispensable and *a priori* conditions for creating internal markets, which in their turn increase the prospect of profit for private investors.

"We are aware of the fact that when capital is risked abroad, it expects to obtain considerable profit, the latter being its justification for the apparent or real risk to which it is subject. As one can note, it is neither pertinent nor exact to say that private investment is going to meet our capital requirements in Bolivia, except perhaps in the fields of the mining and petroleum industries, which have a great appeal to all investors.

"On the other hand, it is interesting to analyze the advantages and disadvantages that the investment of exclusively private capital would bring to the economy of underdeveloped countries. There is no doubt that more capital has been exported from Latin America in the form of profit than has been brought to it. It is therefore evident, from the point of view of the urgent need to obtain capital, common to all our countries, that the remedy of expecting it all to come from private investment is worse than the ills themselves. Foreign private investments that have to take their income to their country of origin and amortize their capital rapidly in order to satisfy the investors are, in spite of themselves, a constant drain on the country.

"All the foregoing leads us to pose the problem of economic cooperation in realistic terms. There does not seem to be any other solution than the granting of loans for development under favorable conditions and terms, on the part of institutions whose essential aim is not to make unlimited profits. When the loans are repaid, the capital assets acquired thereby, i.e., the agricultural and stockraising industries, the hydroelectric plants, and the highways built would remain in the country, and would have the additional advantage of preparing better conditions for possible future private investment.

"It must be added that Bolivia's experience demonstrates that a program of economic cooperation requires something more than the good will of the United States. For example, the feudal system of our agricultural economy renders it unproductive.

". . . None of the achievements of the National Revolution is of greater importance to Bolivia than the Agrarian Reform. Not only has it transformed our agricultural economy, in liberating forces that were hitherto enchained [by] the feudal system, but it has integrated the rural inhabitants into the domestic market, both as providers of food products and as consumers of manufactured goods and services.

". . . Among political topics, none has awakened greater interest than international Communism, and it is not too much to say that we are in danger of losing goodly amounts of work on account of it. Let us not forget that our peoples expect of us something more than a new way to combat Communism—something suitable for improving their lot with respect to welfare and progress.

"Bolivia agrees that international Communism constitutes an intervention in the affairs of America and that one of its characteristics consists in an endeavor to distort for its own ends the genuinely progressive political and social movements of the hemisphere.

"Our experience in this matter is worthy of some attention. We have learned through it that international Communism has no true interest in stating and solving the problems of the country in which it operates. The workers of that party and its local organizations are like pawns in the immense chess game of world politics. They are moved in coordination with and obedience to a plan that is not theirs, the great scope and objectives of which they do not even know most of the time.

". . . We cannot nor should we deceive ourselves as to the attraction that international Communism holds, especially because one of its characteristic traits is to wave as their own the banners that the people hold in highest esteem. Every popular aspiration, every just claim, every protest against exploitation figures prominently in the national programs of international Communism.

"Nevertheless, we should be stopping at the halfway mark if we went [no] further than this in what we are saying. We must go on to find the reasons why international Communism sets itself up as a form of intervention in our affairs and as a threat to our liberties.

"The principal reason has been accurately pointed out in the addresses already delivered here. It lies in the fact that although Communism, like certain diseases, exists potentially in all environments, it develops only in those communities that are favorable to it, and there is nothing more favorable to Communism than collective poverty, oppression, and injustice.

"Consequently, international declarations or resolutions, like measures of domestic suppression, can be only relatively effective as long as there exist conditions of poverty, deep-rooted social injustices, attitudes of indifference, or political regimes that are oppressive and in opposition to the people's will. Where and when such conditions exist, with no one taking the responsibility for correcting them, any solution, any change, however desperate, seems better than the existing state of affairs. Even the mirage of an earthly paradise and perfection that international Communism promises for this world is viewed as possible and acceptable by those who have no alternative hope.

"Furthermore, anti-Communism, as it is usually practiced in our time and in our America, does more to give international Communism prestige and to disseminate it than it does to restrain it. Wherever oppression rarifies the atmosphere of democracy in the name of anti-Communism; wherever every attempt at social and political progress is stifled by violence, under the pretext of its being instigated by Communism; wherever the legitimate claims of labor are defined by employers and governments as a Communist inspired threat to undermine the social order, we can be sure that the attraction of international Communism is increasing by leaps and bounds through the activities of the very ones who claim to be combating it.

"Without defining international Communism, we can describe the characteristics of its agents and organizations: they begin by renouncing, although it may be only to themselves, the land of their birth, and this enables them to act against their own country when their secret leaders order them to do so. Their disciplined squads appear in public showing only the less important members, or under the egis of good-will organizations, the majority of which are composed of people without political experience; and they quietly place their most able men in positions of responsibility in public and private office. In many cases, like that of Bolivia, for example, they form an alliance with the local oligarchies when such a move furthers their objectives.

"But the people now know them, the labor-union leaders and the forward-looking politicians are quickly becoming oriented, and consequently suitable security measures, added to a program of social and economic well-being, will be sufficient to control the danger.

"Nevertheless it seems necessary for this Conference to find appropriate means of security and defense against the agents of international communism, means applicable after each individual case has been specifically examined, so that it should be impossible or at least difficult to make use of them with the sole purpose of maintaining tyranny and exploitation, or of destroying progressive political and labor movements. Care should be taken, especially that the instruments for political defense of the hemisphere should not substitute a potential danger for an immediate one, like intervention in the internal affairs of any country."[4]

Now for the debit side of our balance sheet. Several typical political phenomena stand in the way of de-

[4] Translated by Secretariat, Tenth Inter-American Conference document 128 (English), SP28, March 9, 1954. Original Spanish.

mocracy, such as militarism, or, more properly, *caudillismo*, from the Spanish, which in the past had been deeply imbedded in Latin American history, tradition, and culture. The *caudillo*, or leader, is usually a dynamic and strong-willed person who sees himself as a national leader with a mission that only he is capable of carrying out for the good of the country. Usually the army is diverted from its specific functions and, as an instrument of power, becomes a major force in the country's life. In most cases the *caudillo* is a military man, but not necessarily. The usual procedure for establishing a military dictatorship follows this pattern: army officers in high station overthrow the legitimate government; after a period of strong-armed government by decree, the army man in charge gets himself elected to the presidency by one of two very simple and expedient methods—either he is elected by a hand-picked assembly or congress, or he rigs elections in his favor by eliminating from the race all possible opposition. Governments of this type usually invest a large percentage of their budgets in the armed forces in order to stay in power, and embark in spectacular, hastily planned programs of public works that do not always keep within the limits of the economic capacity of the country. Economic collapse usually brings with it, as a necessary corollary, political collapse. Wherever the economic situation of the country is strong, the dictator is better entrenched. In other cases the typical military dictatorship evolves into a different type with the addition of some new ingredients based on elements of extreme nationalism and native interpretations of fascist doctrines imported from Europe.

But not always have the armed forces served the cause of despotism. On the contrary, they have many times been responsible for preventing the providential type of ruler from perpetuating himself in office. It must be fairly stated that in most cases the armed forces have not divorced themselves from the people by serving as instruments for oppression; they have been the guardians of peace and national dignity as well as the sentinels of continental unity, on guard against enemies from without the hemisphere in accordance with clearly specified obligations of the inter-American system. While in the countries dominated by dictators there is always a growing reaction of hate and fear against the armed forces that have strayed from their sacred mission, in the democracies the army is considered an enlightened institution, deeply respected and loved, constantly contributing to the welfare of the country through many useful activities.

Another type of dictatorship is the paternalistic, which fortunately is rapidly disappearing from the Latin American scene. They begin by overthrowing established governments and once in power convert their country practically into their own private property. They operate under the assumption that their country is not quite ready for true democratic government, and that their system of government is capable of bringing about rapid material progress. Curiously, even though their people are deprived of all liberties, these dictators appear as staunch defenders of democracy at the international table.

Another political reality that should be taken into account is nationalism, which is undoubtedly a force of our times to reckon with, that sometimes becomes more clearly defined and more evident through authentic internal factors and at other times because of international errors and injustices.

Nationalism can be genuine and wholesome if it means patriotism, defense of the country's traditions, its cultural heritage, its language, its folklore, its religion. But it can be harmful and dangerous if it manifests itself in terms of prejudice against everything foreign, as a negation of international life, as an imposition of criteria whether they be ideals or intolerance for all different ideas, or as a solid front against any system that makes possible freedom of examination, freedom of discussion, freedom of action, or free and tolerant debate. Nationalism becomes a dangerous weapon when it tries to annul the individual, harnessing him into ironclad disciplines which makes possible the easy domination of the masses by a few. Then it becomes antidemocratic, because it is inhuman. It becomes a dangerous weapon because under it the people can no longer deliberate, and they suddenly find themselves marching blindly behind their leaders, whatever their intentions.

A well-understood nationalism could be a force on the side of democracy as is the case in the great democratic countries which, without renouncing their own cultural backgrounds and political unity, try to understand the position of others, and at the table of international discussion exchange views and set up organizations for regional defense. This is how international democracy has channelled nationalism into action for the common benefit.

If nationalism is not tolerant of other points of view, it degenerates into totalitarianism. This is a great problem for the democracies to examine because nationalism should be studied, understood and redeemed from dangerous extremes. Communism has taken advantage of the situation and used the extreme manifestations of nationalism against democracy. It is interesting to note that communism is always careful not to oppose nationalistic dictators.

From this brief description of the political map of Latin America one might think that but for a few exceptions the case for democracy is quite hopeless, at least for the time being. The picture is not as bad as it looks. The dictators are usually backed by privileged minorities and the force of arms. Those countries under dictatorial rule are usually under great tensions that cannot be maintained permanently. On the other hand, the large masses of people that have been oppressed, if not simply forgotten, for centuries are beginning to awake to the realization that they have a right to share in the tasks and participate in the fruits that destiny has put in their paths.

In addition to the typical Latin American situations mentioned above, which obstruct the road to democracy, there is a relatively new development that should be taken into account because of its potential importance. Although apparently we all lead a peaceful international life, there actually exists a real psychological state of war on the Latin American front. Without the characteristics of the cold war the situation emerges from conflicting positions and conceptions between the Western democracies and communism. In the offensive of this struggle appear different anti-democratic sectors, both external and internal, in each country. Those forces with experience in infiltration, propaganda and sabotage are deeply interested in deteriorating the relations between Latin America and the United States. In opposition to this menace there is no coherent, overall, well-planned action, and therefore we are actually losing ground to the enemy. It is urgent that Latin America increase its good will and friendship toward the United States; it is vital for the United States to strengthen the front with its closest neighbors, both geographically and historically as well as in destiny. Various factors, fortunately, can help us in this vital struggle. Above all, we constitute a geographical unit, our common histories have just commenced, and we all march along the common road of occidental democracy.

Furthermore, the people of Latin America have a

long-standing democratic tradition. They are fundamentally opposed to the communistic system. Spanish individualism and the old French liberalism are in the background of the political thinking of every Latin American. This, of course, is evident if the democratic form of government shows itself capable of solving the basic problems of the standard of living and the struggle against ignorance and misery which are predominant in great sectors of the population of Latin America. Furthermore, in all the countries, no matter how drastic the suppression of human rights has been by dictators or how totally liberty has been suppressed, there has always been a nucleus, sometimes large and sometimes small, that in the face of tremendous odds and great dangers has kept alive the hope for freedom in the hearts of the people.

Although, as we have outlined, one of the greatest drawbacks for democratic government has been the lack of experience in self-government that goes all the way back to the colonial political system imposed by the mother country, the long experience of over a hundred years of trial and error and the knowledge of what it means to live under regimes of political servitude, plus the fact that during the last few decades the common man in Latin America has gained much ground in improving his standard of living and obtaining conquests of a social nature, have enabled the Latin American to reach the point where he feels that he is ready to intervene directly in the government of his country. The experiment in Ecuador, under extreme conditions, is a vivid reminder that a new era in democratic government can come to all of Latin America because the people are ready for it. An ever-growing number of people from Latin America have visited the United States and have been educated here. They are sincere friends of the United States who realize that much can be borrowed from the United States to bring about an atmosphere of progress in their own countries without any danger to their own cultural values. They represent, however, a minority; and most probably large majorities in their respective countries do not participate in their ideas. Nevertheless, they constitute a nucleus for positive, democratic, anti-totalitarian action in Latin America.

On the other hand, in the United States can be found the necessary elements in the way of talent, resources, institutions, and methods to participate successfully in the psychological battle that must be waged against prejudice and rumors that are cunningly circulated by totalitarians from the right and from the left, from within and from without the hemisphere.

What can be done to strengthen the cause of democracy in Latin America? It is indispensable that action be taken to offset the accusations against the United States that circulate freely in Latin America, accusations like the following: that the United States has reduced her interest in Latin America in favor of increased economic activity in Europe, Asia and, more recently, in Africa; that she favors internal political upheaval in Latin America and that internal continental controversies are prolonged unnecessarily in order to keep Latin America weak and divided; that quotations for Latin American raw materials are kept low in United States markets, while prices of goods manufactured in the United States are constantly rising; that there is a current, even in high places, against the gradual industrialization of Latin America as a future menace to United States industry; that the United States Government prefers to deal with dictators rather than take the trouble to go through the intricacies of democratic government.

Most of these assertions could be done away with by adequate information—not simply propaganda, but comprehensive information based on the truth and on actual United States policy directed to counteract these impressions. This campaign of information should be carried out systematically and intelligently, with an understanding of the people of Latin America, through the press, radio, moving pictures, news agencies, and publishing agencies. Of course, information cannot be the only weapon. It should be synchronized with other programs of cultural exchange as well as technical co-operation, capital investments, and know-how for mutual benefit plus diplomatic action and international agreements in absolute accordance with the basic plan.

There are certain sectors of opinion in Latin America that should be reached in order to counteract efficiently unfavorable propaganda and the deterioration of good relations, which have visibly increased. These are intellectual groups, including writers, artists, professors, and newsmen; labor in its tendencies of the right, left, and center; members of the armed forces; and the church, which is predominantly Catholic in Latin America. These sectors can be reached by using the best elements among their opposite numbers in the United States.

The situation calls for effective action from all quarters. The initiative and responsibility should not rest only on the shoulders of the United States; it should be ours in Latin America as well and should cover various fields, particularly political, economic, and educational, both domestic and international. At the international level it is important to Latin America that the continental jurisdictional system be strengthened, because it guarantees the sovereign existence of each country against inter-continental expansion. Within the universalism of the United Nations we should accentuate the unity of conceptions, of emotions and of action of the people of the Americas.

The Treaty of Reciprocal Assistance, signed by the American States at Rio de Janeiro in 1947, was a great step in advancing inter-American policies and procedures. It imposed the obligation, on each part, to assist any other American state in meeting an armed attack. Aggression against any state is considered aggression against all. This international law imposed upon themselves by twenty-one American republics has replaced the Monroe Doctrine, which was part of the basic international policy of the United States. What was unilateral as a United States obligation alone is now multi-lateral in the Treaty of Reciprocal Assistance. What had been the sole responsibility of the United States today is the collective responsibility of the Western Hemisphere.

The Treaty is applicable in all cases of aggression, whether from within or without the hemisphere; acts of aggression would invoke the same obligation of assistance regardless of their origin. It was unfortunate for my own country that this development of American juridical ordination came about only recently. Some years before, in 1941, Ecuador was the victim of aggression by Peru, which brought about as a consequence an unjust boundary treaty, imposed by the force of arms, while the hemisphere looked on with unbelievable indifference. Proper use of instruments of international actions should be made in order to solve pending local problems which create international tensions.

A major aspiration of all the countries of the hemisphere is to strengthen and put to practical use the inter-American system. I have selected remarks made at Caracas by the Foreign Ministers of Mexico and Chile, which reflect clearly the thinking of Latin America today.

Luis Padilla Nervo, Foreign Minister of Mexico, said:

"From its origin, up to the time of the Bogotá Conference, Pan Americanism represents an effort to create and improve the standards of our international life. In its first phase it refers to the will of the members of the American community to set the foundation for the solution of their differences by peaceful means, to adjust their relations within limits of mutual respect. As a consequence, the principle of non-intervention and juridical equality of the states was formally consecrated. Later on, the war, which for the second time in this century divided the world into two antagonistic camps, drove us to organize a regional system of collective security within the framework of the United Nations. Finally, at the end of the great struggle our conscience was assailed by the fact that measures of a political nature are not sufficient to prevent war; we realized that the causes of conflict should be eliminated at their origin, by combating misery and ignorance. This is the phase we have just started: the one concerned with positive cooperation in economic and social matters.

". . . We believe that at the Conference we should apply our efforts to put into practice effectively and sincerely, without doubts, the standards we have created. What should give life to our resolutions is to convert into more tangible realities the principles stated in the Charter of Bogotá. This meeting may well be the supreme test by which the American community is strengthened, if it has the courage to put into practice the ideals it has proclaimed. Otherwise it fails as an authentic family of nations. The organization created five years ago will justify its existence to the extent that we are able to live up to its principles now.

". . . We are deeply concerned over the manner in which Point V of the Agenda has been stated ('intervention of international communism in the American republics') and we consider it a duty to our solidarity to expose, from this tribune, our points of view.

". . . Because we share with the other nations of America the same democratic determinations, we are prepared to offer our participation to any program that may arise for the defense and development of democracy, only under the condition that such a program should not undermine the great juridical principles that are the basis for the very existence of continental solidarity: non-intervention, juridical equality, respect for the sovereignty of the states and their political independence, which implies the recognition of the right that each nation has to adopt the form of government that it desires.

"We cannot accept the idea, which has been expressed on several occasions, that the mission to protect our institutions is no longer a matter of exclusive national jurisdiction of our respective governments, but has become a matter of international nature to be susceptible of collective action. If we accepted this doctrine we would be invading the private domain of the states and, hence, would be violating both the Bogotá and San Francisco Charters, which prohibit individual or collective intervention in the internal affairs of the states, and we would be converting our organization into a super-national tribunal with a right to judge our institutions and regulate the democratic sentiments of our governments.

". . . Our program of action should be to defend democracy without imparing its effective practice, to protect our institutions without curtailing liberty and respect for human rights, and to strengthen continental solidarity without belittling sovereignty and independence of the states. We can and should develop this program by the application of methods and procedures worthy of our time, far, fortunately, from the inquisition and the efforts that have always failed to regiment the conscience and the mind of humanity."[5]

The Chilean Foreign Minister, Tobías Barrios Ortíz, said:

"America has obtained unity in matters of a political and juridical nature and considerable progress has been achieved in social and cultural affairs.

"Unfortunately the economic-financial balance sheet does not give the same feeling of faith and optimism.

"During the period between the First Inter-American Conference and this reunion in Caracas, we find impressive differences in the living conditions of the people of America, an uneven use of natural resources, and a difference in appraisal, sometimes arbitrary and discriminatory, of the national efforts in many countries.

[5] Translated by Galo Plaza and Alexander Heard from Inter-American Conference document 124 (Spanish), SP27, March 8, 1954. Original Spanish.

"In summary, in all the broad field of economic and financial activity, the inter-American system has not yet been able to cooperate towards solving the grave problems that affect our countries and reflect painfully in the standard of living of our people.

"In other geographical regions evident progress can be found in the coordination of their economic possibilities, of their production and their commerce. We also find that as regional units they have received opportune and efficient international assistance.

"The prosperity of others that is translated into well-being of their people gratifies us, but at the same time leaves us in a deep state of uncertainty that should lead us to the necessity to study seriously and definitely what is happening to the inter-American system, with the unity of the hemisphere, with the concept of solidarity in everything political, juridical and cultural, but so modest in practical results in seeking common prosperity.

"We are united by geography, by history, and we face common dangers; however, everything gives the impression that we have been abandoned in the hard struggle for economic development and in the necessity to give to our national communities the opportunities of work and well-being they deserve.

". . . Examining the economic situation in general, we can speak of our own experience in inter-American commerce; what has really happened to raw materials, in contradiction to the theories of international commerce in the case of the so-called strategic materials; the true volume of flow of private capital and the continental drought as far as public capital is concerned; how our products are transported and how the lines of communications are controlled; and how contradictory is the development of colonial economies in comparison to the disloyal competition that Latin America receives.

"The present Conference gives us the opportunity to face these grave problems and seek, in common, urgent and practical solutions.

"We should not satisfy ourselves with discussions, no matter how interesting we find the interchange of ideas. These problems have been studied in the past. Possible solutions, in general terms, are already known. What is lacking is action, the firm desire to help ourselves in America. For this reason it is fundamental that we adopt concrete decisions in economic and financial matters. It is necessary that we should know if we are or are not to expect cooperation in order to complement our national efforts, if on the difficult road ahead we are alone or accompanied, and if the wellbeing of our people is a national problem or one of continental concern.

". . . The Chilean government has adopted a clearcut, anti-communist position and our points of view on the subject have been stated in numerous and solemn occasions with the only reservation that in fighting communism individual liberties should not be curtailed nor should it be an excuse for intervention in the internal affairs of a country.

"But it is not enough to combat the subversive activities of international communism by police methods of an internal or international nature, or by resolutions or declarations at inter-American conferences. The breeding grounds for the communist germ should be done away with, that is, poverty and ignorance of the people. Communism is an ally of sadness, hardship and pain, it cannot bloom in prosperous and happy nations"[6]

Action of an economic nature would include well-planned programs to assist democratic countries to solve their problems with efficiency. Capital investment for a human and democratic destiny should be the slogan. Action should be taken to improve the standard of living of the great masses, for poverty is a breeding ground for communism; to strengthen the middle class, which is the stabilizing element of democracy; to make adequate use of natural resources, and see that raw materials receive fair treatment; to encourage well-planned industrialization; and to eliminate the customs barriers as a means to increase the purchase of the elements of civilization, the manufactured goods of United States industry, by the people of Latin America. The purchasing capacity of the Latin American market could thus be multiplied several times for mutual benefit.

[6] Translated by Galo Plaza and Alexander Heard from Inter-American Conference document 75 (Spanish), SP15, March 3, 1954. Original Spanish.

Not much could be achieved without a corresponding educational program in order to defend democratic ideals by conviction, not by imposition. Education of the masses in democracy should be our goal, so that it could filter downward beyond their leaders.

The role that youth should play should be greatly increased by inspiring the new generation with faith in the kind of democracy that our century requires. It should be done in terms of an awareness of struggle against adverse factors rather than against groups of human beings. Greater emphasis should be placed on travel for study, on free discussion, on free exchange of publications, and on the ever-present reality of the interdependence of the world in which we live. Better knowledge of our respective history and geography is needed; offensive remarks and erroneous information in textbooks should be done away with. And, above all, the greatest need is for a more clearly defined spiritual expression of the role of the United States in continental destiny.

If the United States desires a frank and complete expression of the feeling of Latin America she has to go no further than to analyze the points of view set forth at the Tenth Inter-American Conference at Caracas. As the results of the Conference are being studied and evaluated, voices of skepticism can be heard, coming from different quarters throughout the hemisphere, from those who hope for more concrete results and from those who seldom fail to take advantage of an opportunity to criticize any effort to bring about a greater cooperation between the two Americas.

Personally, I do not share these pessimistic views; I do not consider the Conference a failure. I would rather say it has been an expression of the fact that the countries of Latin America have come of age, if not in obtaining solutions to their problems, at least in the way they have analyzed and set them forth.

No doubt, what the Latin American delegates told the United States delegation concerning economic matters was by far the most important aspect of the Conference. Never before had the representatives of Latin America presented their case at the international table with better use of figures, statistics, and conclusions born from studies made by international organizations and based on plans for technical assistance and planning of national economies. The influence of a new generation of economists in government and central bank circles is evident in economic planning, as in the studies of natural resources and of markets and prices. These are the only means of finding the road to progress.

The United States Delegation at Caracas must have found much interesting information set forth in firm but cordial terms by their brothers and friends from the rest of the hemisphere. Latin America did not ask for handouts; they asked for fair treatment at the international market in the fixing of prices and the trend of investments. For this they have already established conditions as attractive as possible, short only of privileges above those granted to domestic capital. They championed the cause of free enterprise; they asked to have a part in determining prices for those items produced by them. Today this is a matter of unilateral decisions, which imposes upon them reduction in prices and in production, and limits their markets, practices which they believe are not prevalent in the case of other allies of the United States. They finally submitted for study the problems of customs barriers and double taxation, the main obstacles to an active and friendly economic development of the hemisphere for the benefit of all concerned.

These are the reasons why the resolution to convoke a Conference of Ministers of Economy in 1954[7] to deal fully with the problems that were submitted at Caracas constitutes a splendid opportunity for the United States to improve its relations with the people and the governments of Latin America.

If a blueprint is taken to that Conference by the United States with concrete solutions in administrative, legislative, and private fields, and if there is a firm in-

[7] The Caracas Conference decided to hold an economic conference in Rio de Janeiro. The Conference took place in November, 1954. Secretary of the Treasury George Humphrey headed the U. S. delegation. This meeting did not contribute much to the cause of Pan Americanism; however, progress was made. Probably the most significant was President Eisenhower's request to Congress to establish the International Finance Corporation, as a one hundred million dollar supplement to the World Bank, for lending to private enterprisers rather than governments. The President also asked Congress to lighten taxation on U. S. firms operating in Latin America. Both these steps were taken in accordance with promises made at Rio.

tention to approach and liquidate the discrepancies already stated at Caracas, the unity of the continent would be greatly strengthened, at a time when unity within the hemisphere is a major issue for the United States as a world power.

If this is the outcome of the forthcoming economic conference we will be able to show a united front to Soviet imperialism and tell them clearly that their false doctrines have no place on American soil where human welfare based on a fair and just understanding of our people is the best expression of a life of dignity and democracy.

From what has been said we can conclude that, whatever the limitations, the barriers in the hemisphere or the undermining action from without, democracy is evidently on the march, not an inert, static expression of democracy, but a dynamic formula constantly in the process of evolution. Its eighteenth century definition no longer holds true today. It must express itself as a new, up-to-date conception fitting the twentieth century, at the dawn of the atomic era.

Democracy is no longer the responsibility of individuals as such, or of nations separately; it is the responsibility of convening efforts in our interdependent world. Our errors in Latin America are no longer our own alone, from now on they will be the collective responsibility of all the hemisphere.